God Thoughts of a Lesser Mind on a Higher Plane

God Thoughts of a Lesser Mind on a Higher Plane

Kathie F. Bell

iUniverse, Inc.
New York Bloomington Shanghai

God Thoughts of a Lesser Mind on a Higher Plane

Copyright © 2008 by Kathie F. Bell

All rights reserved. No part of this book may be used or reproduced by any means, graphic, electronic, or mechanical, including photocopying, recording, taping or by any information storage retrieval system without the written permission of the publisher except in the case of brief quotations embodied in critical articles and reviews.

iUniverse books may be ordered through booksellers or by contacting:

iUniverse
1663 Liberty Drive
Bloomington, IN 47403
www.iuniverse.com
1-800-Authors (1-800-288-4677)

Because of the dynamic nature of the Internet, any Web addresses or links contained in this book may have changed since publication and may no longer be valid.

Some material was copy written by poetry.com

ISBN: 978-0-595-47746-3

Printed in the United States of America

Contents

PREFACE	ix
SIMPLE REFLECTIONS	1
JESUS THE CHRIST	2
AWAKENED BY GOD	3
GOD	4
TO KNOW GOD	5
WHERE IS GOD?	6
IT'S ALL GOOD	7
IF YOU CAN'T BE HAPPY WHERE YOU ARE	9
THE GIFT	10
THANKS AGAIN	11
KNOW THYSELF AND THEN BE SURE	12
DREAM	13
EXPRESSIONS IN TRUTH	14
WHY?	15
I LOVE MY FEAR TO DEATH	16
TRUE LOVE ALWAYS LOVES	17
LAW	18
WHO AM I REALLY?	21

JESUS SAID	22
MY TRUTH	23
ARE YOU READY?	24
SEARCHING FOR GOD	25
GODS GRACE	26
NOW	27
THANK YOU GOD	28
THE PEARLY WHITE GATES	29
CHANGING LOOKS	30
BEING IN THE LOVE OF CHRIST	32
SEE ME	34
FEAR GOD? NEVER	35
WINNER	36
BE STILL AND GOD WILL	38
YOU CAN NEVER FAIL AT LOVE	40
WHERE LORD?	41
REMEMBER?	42
LET IT GO	43
CREATE SOMETHING GOOD	44
BEAUTY	45
RELIGION OR SPIRIT	46
ABUNDANCE	48
THINK RIGHT	50
IN THE PALM OF ONE HAND	51

LOST AND THEN FOUND 52
THINK IT THROUGH 54
READY OR NOT 57
THE CASE OF LOVE 58
TREASURE 59
TRUTH 60
YOU LIVE ONCE 61
A LIFE WELL SPENT 62
JUST IN CASE 63
TALKING TO GOD 64
EVERYTHING I AM IS YOURS 65
666 MYTHS 66
JESUS I BELIEVE IN YOU 67

PREFACE

Kathie Bell self made child of God

I call myself self-made because God is the one who equipped me with everything I would need for this life. It was up to me to explore what he placed in me. As the story of my life has unfolded before my eyes I see the truth placed in me from the beginning. God loves each one of us so much there are not enough words or stories to tell. We are told the Bible is a collection of books. Well friend, we are the next book. Everyone of us is a book of the Bible. We are that 67th living epistle. We are in the book of life, God never stopped speaking. It's ok to read someone else's testimony (life account) but it is up to us to start living and drawing out of our own life account. God has deposited everything we need to complete the whole Bible and that does include you. We've opened our mind to interpretations of what others know to be true about God, but now is the time to open our whole self to God. We won't discard someone else's opinion, we'll just be living our own truth and purpose. Say right now God what do you say about me and then let God unravel the masterpiece he thinks about you. The world will be a better place, you will be honored and God will be once again Glorified.

I dedicate this collections of my thought life to my family, not forgetting my oldest brother Jack Blevins following is the summary thought appropriate for his life.

Jackie Ray Blevins
October 5,1954–February 1,2007
Integrity

Jackie used to always say I'm Jack Blevins I am a perfectionist. Some of us laughed some criticized some of us thought he was just crazy. When I think of Jackie I think of the parable Jesus told, (Jesus being my other brother). The story of the seeds that were given, some fell on stony ground some in weeds some the birds ate, some on good ground. I believe Jackie was good ground. What he didn't know because no one had ever told him was that a seed of strength and integrity was put in him. When the enemy came he didn't come for anything, but that seed. He came to kill, steal, and destroy, that seed God had planted. But we say let every other manifested thing in my life be a lie but only God's word true. Jackie was cut into deep for that seed. However he did not give it up. He claimed it to the very end. Do it right or don't do it at all. Many wrong bad misfortune and terrible things happened to Jackie, Jackie still believed in perfection. He'd say Kathie or the name of one of my other brother or sisters, if you're not gonna do it right, there's no sense in doing it. Jackie was not a perfect man, but he believed in perfection. We know there is only one who was perfect. He said if you believe in me you won't be ashamed. He believed in the character of Jesus-perfection. He believed in doing things right no matter what was done to him. To believe in integrity is to believe in the character of God. Jackie expressed that part of God's character through his whole life. He worked hard not only one job, but he worked two jobs. And he did his job right displaying and expressing the character of God. Some people asked if he had the Holy Ghost? Some may have just thought it. Well here is you answer, an apple doesn't produce oranges and a person cannot express God if God hasn't first impressed the person. This is the evidence, no I didn't hear Jackie speak in any languages I couldn't understand, but he expressed his desire for perfection and he exampled integrity. He resembled his father, his creator, and his elder brother. It cost him his life here, but Jesus said if any man give up his life for my sake he will not be without. Jackie loved God and God loved him back.

SIMPLE REFLECTIONS

Imagine a God in all his splendor

Imagine a God in all his glory

Imagine a God in all his magnificence

Imagine a God in all his fullness

His only Desire to leave all

So he might die for me to live

I'm so glad my God isn't just my

Imagination

JESUS THE CHRIST

God being in the form of man,

came many times before.

But only one man, Jesus

knew this truth for sure.

He passed the test,

and takes the time,

to show and tell,

God in everyone.

AWAKENED BY GOD

The wisdom of God is like the ray of sunshine,

As it infiltrates my being it brings me to life,

With every sense awakened,

I smell the beauty of flowers,

I feel the depth of texture,

I taste the season of goodness,

I hear the splendor of creation,

And I can see the love of God.

GOD

Before time started one day

Beyond measure in either way

In spite of nothing

Because of love

Underneath it all

And on top of everything else

God's a genius.

TO KNOW GOD

To know about God,

is someone else's opinion.

To know God is truth

WHERE IS GOD?

I am but a breath away

from the presence of God.

Whether just a thought away;

or I speak out his name,

In the midst of a noisy day,

in the silent prayer,

either way,

a second here or a minute there,

God is present and very near.

IT'S ALL GOOD

Inspired by Joy

Intrigued by Love

Enabled by Passion

Encouraged by Freedom

I welcome each day with

Intended enthusiasm and

Expectancy of all the good

Life has to offer

And I am rarely disappointed.

Oh God it's you who loves us into eternity,

it's only our painful attempts to hold on here,

that causes us to hurt in the process.

IF YOU CAN'T BE HAPPY WHERE YOU ARE

HOW CAN YOU POSIBLY BE HAPPY WHERE YOU ARE NOT?

THE GIFT

Thank you God for this precious gift,

I'll treasure it for the rest of my life.

When I see the whole day through

with joy and wonderfulness

others will often begin to see

this beautiful gift you gave to me.

They have one too

I'm almost sure

you're word in me

promises the whole world.

The gift I treasure with great delight,

is the gift of life; no I mean eternal

Life.

THANKS AGAIN

Life in the middle of the day can almost seem

like you're just going around again. Give God thanks

as we go around again and again everyday.

KNOW THYSELF AND THEN BE SURE

As I came to know myself; I now know more than I ever dreamed. And that's how it happened. I dreamed I saw me and a rainbow. As I reached out into the rainbow, I was exhilarated with passion and joy as never before. The colors were amazing, and full of energy. The purple so exquisite and pure with magic, the blue with calming effects that were magnetizing, green coming in waves of abundance filled with excitement and joy, yellow most enveloping and warm, orange inviting and charming, red was just bursting with creativity and power esteeming me higher and higher. As I was soaring into the unknown I realized it wasn't unknown anymore, but someplace I had been before. Taking a closer look I noticed this rainbow coming out of me, and I knew this was home for me. I found myself in the colors of life that I thought we gone forever. I forgave me for living at a lower consciousness that was never intended for me. I in my lower awareness had become my greatest stepping stone to the truth. Today I promise just as God promised Noah so many years before, I will never destroy my lower self again with anything. As I send out doves with requests to the universe, I am expecting to receive full notice that it is time for me to return to the life God intended me to live. I will joy in the rest of my life.

DREAM

I get so excited watching my dreams

come to pass.

However I have never felt more alive,

than when I physically engage

in the actual dream. Act it out.

EXPRESSIONS IN TRUTH

When I let God impress me, then I can express him.

The world is then exposed to the knowledge of God.

In unity we become one, as only love is shown,

fear and doubt flee the light, only truth remains.

We can then enter into the pearly gates of Heaven,

and all is well.

WHY?

Reasoning and Purpose

Are by far the best

For it's in my purpose

That I reason all the rest.

I LOVE MY FEAR TO DEATH

I watch my fears dissolve when I face them,

embrace the truth about them, and

love them to death; remembering perfect

Love casts out all fear.

TRUE LOVE ALWAYS LOVES

There was a time I absolutely loved God and of course God absolutely loved me back. Then there was the time I misunderstood God and of course God absolutely loved me back. And then the time I hated God and of course God absolutely loved me back. Yes, even the time I rebelled and ran from God and God absolutely loved me back. Now I have come to know, appreciate, worship, respect, and absolutely love God; because God absolutely loved me back.

LAW

Love At Work in me,

becomes the intent

in word and deed.

I see myself as only right,

God too sees me in perfect light.

Let Love At Work in you

be in all you say and do.

You know you will be right

As god sees you in perfect light.

Love At Work in us

Creates more love and trust

We then start living right

God exposing all of us in light.

Continuing to look back into my past,

only reminds me of how I used to look

forward to my future … Oh yeah that's today.

LIVE RIGHT NOW!!!!!!!!!!!!!!!!!!!!!!!!!

WHO AM I REALLY?

When I turn my focus on God,

I am centering my lower consciousness,

with my higher esteemed spirit.

All resistance flees and I soar into

The wonderment of the unknown

I am filled with the joy and bewilderment of a child

As I start to play in the universe of Love,

I am granted access because of my fathers position,

The creator of everything that ever was and will be.

JESUS SAID

And Jesus said "you should love the law of God with all your heart (*with your whole life, life is in the heart*), with all your mind (*with your whole awareness, conscientiously on purpose loving*), with all your soul (*in spirit or inspired enthusiastically and creatively*) and with all your strength (*tenaciously or persevering with the intent that guides you*). There is no greater law than this. The one closest to it is Love (*accept, respect, give to, pray for, be compassionate to, forgive, or give for*) your neighbor as yourself (*if you do the first law you will be loving to yourself because the law of God is really stating the law of good; so then be good to yourself in life, consciously, enthusiastically, persevering to your goals, dreams and desires, and then help somebody else realize this*). These are the greatest laws of God."

MY TRUTH

Only when I drift into thoughts of doubt and fear

do I become afraid and lost.

Lost in a world looking to others

who are lost in the daily routines of nothingness,

until I remember my fathers house;

one with peace and harmony.

When I return to my truths of Love and joy

then I am home.

I have been lost many times;

but I am only found once,

and that is in oneness with God.

My times of found are only when I realize (remembering my TRUTH)

I AM God's child and no thing can harm me.

ARE YOU READY?

Are you ready?

Maybe let's see.

I think I'm ready,

but can you read me?

Ready starts off with read

don't you know?

Reading myself first,

before starting the show;

If I understand, what I read,

I'll always be ready

in word and in deed.

SEARCHING FOR GOD

Looking for God in the flowers,

I see dandelions brightly show off.

Listening for God in the rain.

I hear GOD loud and clear in the thunder.

Exploring God in life situations

I am reveals God in me.

Imagining then, God in me,

exposes the Glory of God through me,

What a wonderful life.

GODS GRACE

G oodness
R eplenishing
A ll
C reation
E veryday

So then God's goodness replenishing all creation everyday is sufficient.

NOW

N ext
O pportunity
W as

That is how fast now is happening in this time era. We are living in a much faster pace. The energy is much higher now than ever before. So if you want to do something great or noble you had better do it now. Before you can hardly finish the word; the word is over, and means the moment has already passed. We are evolving into a different sphere. Time will seem to fly, but in reality there is no such thing as time. There are a lot of moments in eternity but there is only one eternity; in this moment right now. Where will you spend eternity? I hope to spend mine in the present right now.

THANK YOU GOD

Thank you God for my vision today,

I feel your love in every way.

Thanking you for the desires of my heart,

today, I decide the way to start.

Even the truth that seeks me out

reveals your presence without a doubt.

Seeing this evidence of your love so strong,

makes everyday flow right along.

How can I forget the good you create;

when I am surrounded by such excellent fate?

Thank you God I love you dear

I'll always remember you're forever near.

THE PEARLY WHITE GATES

Look at that pearly white gate,

have you seen such a site?

Of course you have,

the very one you use to bite.

We all have this pearly white gate,

given to us by God for only our fate.

Next time you start to show,

remember to smile, it's the gate you know.

You decide heaven or hell,

by how you open this gate on you face,

Let only joy, peace, and love dwell in that space.

for that is the gate that determines the place.

CHANGING LOOKS

If you want to know me,

look at me now.

Don't wait for tomorrow,

I'll be different somehow.

We can grow in love,

or part in peace;

either way it will work out,

that's for sure without a doubt.

Each day starts in me something new,

and even does the same for you.

Don't you see it's God in us all,

And so everything in us, all good.

BEING IN THE LOVE OF CHRIST

Its hoping in love that frightens us still,

while being in love makes heaven so real.

I love the feelings that go along

with being in love, just like the song.

You don't have to hope, pray, or look,

just beware you are in the book.

The end always comes soon enough,

it's the stories that make up the love.

Be just as content on the page you are now,

in no time at all the story changes somehow.

It's true for every soul that's here

there really is no-thing at all to fear.

We all live happily ever after,

so be in love and enjoy the laughter.

This is how every tale will end,

in the light and love of Jesus our friend.

SEE ME

Can you see me can't you tell,

I've been with Jesus

All night through hell.

He saved me once he saves me still,

Believe you me I know he's real.

Shows me the father,

makes me believe.

in a wonderful future,

I'm about to receive.

I love you Jesus,

I love the Christ,

for showing me the truth

about my life.

FEAR GOD? NEVER

Heavenly father how can I please you still?

In my weakness you bring me life and will,

In sorrow you instill me with great joy,

In my loneliness you bring the same, even more.

In my worst fear you brought peace and light,

In my biggest mistake your presence alone secured me tight.

How can I now fear this one so great.

When anytime I have failed; only with kindness do you relate.

I LOVE YOU GOD!   Kathie

WINNER

If God, Jesus, and the Holy Spirit all agree

about me; why am I arguing with them?

Majority always wins. Let go and let God.

BE STILL AND GOD WILL

In the name of God I am who I am, fully centered in the presence I know,

the truth of what Jesus told me.

My mind says to belong I need to conform to the world;

God said greater is what he put in me that anything in the world.

My eyes say I need to lookout for safety;

God says to look within for the kingdom.

My ears say my worth depends upon what others say and think about me;

God says every word he said about me is only truth and not one word would return void.

My heart says I've been hurt and I feel afraid;

God says he will never leave or forsake me.

My body says I am tired of fighting for life;

God says be still and know I am the way, truth, and the life.

My intuition says fear can cause me to be unable to get it right;

God says I am saved with his righteousness and his perfect love will cast out all my fear.

The world says I am not exactly what was expected;

God says he formed me before the foundations of the world.

Religious leaders say I am a sinner and of no use to God or anyone, without their approval;

God says I know the thoughts I have toward you; Thoughts to prosper you, heal you, cleanse you, and restore you to wholeness once and for all.

Then Jesus said it is finished, just believe; and I say

I think I will God's will.

YOU CAN NEVER FAIL AT LOVE

Oh so you say you can't find Love,

be still and let love find you.

Love is always looking for another prospect;

another soul to save, another wound to heal,

another mind to expand, another bridge to build,

another faith to stretch, another heart to mend,

another ego to break, another life to win.

Love will find you rest assured,

For this is truly in Gods own word.

WHERE LORD?

Lord tell me where to stand and I will not fall,

listen from me so I can hear,

speak through me so I can be,

look into my eyes to behold you glory,

enable my mind to glimpse the almighty,

feel me with you presence, so I can know,

and be found whole in the universe for eternity.

REMEMBER?

Before you came here,

you were already here.

Before you go there,

you'll be there too.

Before you know who you are,

love already knew you.

So open up you heart and let God be good through you.

LET IT GO

Let it go

and feel the love

You came from God,

you'll go back for more.

I'll see you again,

and this I know for sure.

God in me is God in you,

This is the plan forevermore.

Be all God made in you.

Just be you.

Just be you.

CREATE SOMETHING GOOD

I arrange words to say something good,

since I was created I am sure I should.

God created me and called me good,

I create placement of words,

to be easily understood.

In lay mans terms God loves you too,

just open your eyes see what you do.

If it doesn't look right,

Don't worry or fret, just

change your mind to fix the sight.

See what I mean when good does call,

for surely it frees us, to become good in all.

BEAUTY

Beauty recognized from the inside,

reflects the presence of God outward,

and the whole world witnesses it,

The key word being whole.

RELIGION OR SPIRIT

Religion is exclusive in that you must yield to the conclusion of the leader to be accepted. Spiritual is inclusive of all in the material and invisible world here or not yet here leader or no leader for anyone who asks.

ABUNDANCE

It is my natural state
It is my inherited right
To acknowledge and accept my divinity.

My natural state I was born, mercy and grace follow me all the days of my life.
My inherited right is because of what Jesus did. I don't have to fast 40 days or go to an old rugged cross because Jesus already did the ground work. He uncovered the truth. It's is accepting in faith this truth that Jesus told me that sets me free from the lie. I am of the father. To have access to an inheritance someone has to die. I couldn't inherit the truth about the Holy Spirit (spark of God the whole) with out Jesus leaving. It was his righteousness (right thinking or acknowledgement of truth) that saved me.
To acknowledge my divinity, God said I thought of you before I laid the foundations of the world.
Consider the ocean, one drop examples the Holy Spirit by it's self; the natural state are the creatures of the ocean. The ocean as whole is God. Abundance is
My natural state
My inherited right
To acknowledge and accept the truth of my divinity is just life more abundant.

Which is what Jesus came to make known for all humanity. We three are one is truth for everyone.

One drop is as the whole (same quality)

Creatures are of the whole (live move and have their being).

The ocean of itself who can fully understand or who has captured it totally? Better yet, consider even the bigger picture the whole universe who has all it's answers or who can know the boundaries. We are all one in and of the one. We are of the whole.

THINK RIGHT

Don't be fooled whatsoever a man sows that he will also reap, God is not mocked. If you sow to the sinful nature which states I have missed the mark that is the lifestyle you will lead. If you sow to the spirit which says I am full of God power and I have eternity to prove it you will lead that life style. You choose to day; to think which one you want to think (or whom do you want to serve). So be it unto you. As a person thinks so they become.

IN THE PALM OF ONE HAND

Sit up and take notice

I am is pure inclusive,

so then the crutch of,

racism, is no longer,

of use to anyone dead or alive.

LOST AND THEN FOUND

When I try to find my way,

I get into such a mess,

When I think to find Gods way,

my path is made straight and clear.

THINK IT THROUGH

Everybody's talking about it but only some are listening to it.

Very few are looking for it and even less are expecting it

It can't be seen from the Whitehouse

It can't be seen on your television

It can't be seen on your job

It can't be seen in the street

It can't be seen in your family

It can't be seen even at your church

But it is happening right now. This world is changing

so fast sometimes I can't keep up, and yet so subtle I can't put my finger on it

It's unavoidable

It's predictable

It's unpreventable

it's bound to happen

It's unstoppable

It's immeasurable

It's undeniable

It is the power of destiny

And we all have it

One day or another.

As I thought about the different ways, means and years involved with my search for God, I started to wonder if I was trying to know true appreciation for God, or just maneuvering another process, inciting a new for of manipulation to support my (intelligent) bloated ego. To really love God I need to trust that everything is working for my good, so the need to have it or even see my way as right is simply ego in it's most disguising form yet. Search my heart oh God and know me.

READY OR NOT

If you're ever offered the chance for a ride on truth

Do it with eyes wide open,

Mouth tightly shut,

Ears perked for the sound of music

Heart emptied of all past experiences

Mind ready for the next best time of your natural life.

THE CASE OF LOVE

Every time we have occasion or opportunity to be offended, we are really given a call to be a witness for the case of love. Especially by those in the body of Christ. Jesus said Blessed is he who is not offended in me. If we are who we say we are and we say we are Christ's and in the Christian way Blessed are we, when we don't recognize or receive what we consider to be offensive from another.

Most of the time when someone hurts us it is not them hurting us so much as it is feelings of remembrance (*old wounds that are sensitive when bumped into by another*). We now have the opportunity to turn to God for healing. We can't really go to God and tell him someone hit me, because God didn't create hits, so when God doesn't respond or we don't think he's responding we get disappointed. When we go to God and say God so and so hurt me with words, the only words from God are good, the only way God responds is with good words and with Love. We don't want to respond with love so we get mad and we tend to blame and try to shift the responsibility on to another, but God will give us another opportunity to respond (be a witness and testify in the case of love). Don't be discouraged Love always wins. That's what is meant when the scripture states they'll know you are the true sons of God. God looks and we are witnessing in the trial of love and winning. Seeing himself (*God always knows himself*), he states my beloved in whom **I AM** well pleased. When we start mirroring God as he really is he sees himself, is pleased, and we are blessed.

TREASURE

The treasures in life

Everyday in me start.

The treasures of Love

Increasing my heart

The treasures of God

I can see so clear,

Treasures of goodness

As eternal and very near.

TRUTH

Truth awakens the soul within me and I come alive enthusiastic and ready to live. Truth also reveals the divine nature of I am as I look for the same in others I feel connected . Truth uncovers God in me creating more good as a testimony for love. Truth presents who I am to the world as I express God presence within: I impress others . Truth becomes my existence in right now while in this awareness I rise to the occasion presented . Truth frees me to stay in oneness of God as I go into eternity I am know forever and this is the truth.

YOU LIVE ONCE

Time only happens once in a while

You can get it today

Or lay stacked in a pile.

Why wonder on some small cue

Start living your life just for you.

God will love you just the same

If you fail there is no one else to blame.

You just get up brush yourself off good

Live the happy and joyful life you should.

A LIFE WELL SPENT

Spend every minute of life you're given,
never wasting any of it.
That doesn't mean try and save it,
it means live like there's no tomorrow.
Spend some!!!!
Give some!!!!
And if there's any saving to do let the father do the saving; you were created
to live, laugh, love, and enjoy.
When you complete these simple tasks
God the father lives, laughs, loves, and enjoys.

A life well spent and not wasted is one of the joys of the father. Not saved and buried in self righteousness from fear, or judgment, but well spent; using all of your talents and learning new ones. Live full and bold with worthiness that comes only from over exposure to grace.

The joy of the father isn't saving one's life,
rather a life well spent as true expression.
Spending and not wasting your life
is expanding joy, for this gift from God.
Enjoy your life and let
God enjoy watching you.

JUST IN CASE

I want it to be known throughout the whole universe,

I WANT MY CAKE AND EAT IT TOO!

And just in case anybody…..anybody at all
doesn't want their cake,

I LIKE CAKE!!!!!!!!!!!!!!!!

I am just bold enough to believe what Jesus said "I came so you can live life in abundance". Or "I came so you can have your cake and eat it too." What's the point of having your own cake if you can't eat and enjoy it too. Or simply wanting cake and not having it, or thinking I can't have it. I choose today to believe I can have my cake; and eat it too. I accept this truth, and if for any reason you can't or don't want to,

I LIKE CAKE!!!!!!!!!!!!!!!!!!!

P S Notice my hand is held high.

TALKING TO GOD

If you've already talked to God today, then you

know we're related, right?

EVERYTHING I AM IS YOURS

When do you dream,

only in sleep?

Or do you dream,

while fully awake?

Sleep is quiet consciousness,

while awake; full consciousness

aware of itself, headed

to the open road of living.

Coming and going

from here to there.

I've got everything in excess

And all to spare.

666 MYTHS

The number that scares most people is one they hold onto everyday with consistency and determination. The number for man is 6, so then 666 just represents me, myself, and I. It is the thought of separateness and ego that selfishly blinds me to the ***truth***. No government will force me to wear this number on my head or in my hand. It will appear to be there because; I create and govern my own space. I work with my hands making money to satisfy my own wants or I am thinking with my head of how I can make more money to gratify the desire for more material possession. It's all about me, myself, and I. If I continue on this path, it is self-destructive for sure, because when we cut ourselves off from the source we die. What did Jesus say, I am the vine you are the branch. God is our source and everyone else is our re-source. We must stay with the whole; growing, expanding, and branching out are part of the plan, but not to be cut off from the vine. To "thine own self be true," God is at the core of your being. Be true. Agree with God and good will come to you. Agree with good and God will come to you.

JESUS I BELIEVE IN YOU

Jesus I believe in you,

I believe in what you said was true.

You said you were the son of God,

And that I am also too.

Jesus I believe in you,

in everything you say and do

Because you were the son of God

Lets me know that I can too.

978-0-595-47746-3
0-595-47746-1

Printed in the United States
108372LV00004B/524/P